T0151404

PICTURES

of the gone world

LAWRENCE FERLINGHETTI

60TH ANNIVERSARY EDITION

CITY LIGHTS BOOKS
San Francisco

Library of Congress Cataloging-in-Publication Data
Ferlinghetti, Lawrence.
  [Poems. Selections]
 Pictures of the gone world / Lawrence Ferlinghetti. — 60th
anniversary edition.
     pages ; cm. — (City Lights pocket poets series ; 1)
  ISBN 978-0-87286-690-4 (hardcover)
 1. Beat generation—Poetry. I. Title.
  PS3511.E557A6 2015
  811'.54—dc23
                                    2015035461

City Lights Books are published at the City Lights Bookstore
261 Columbus Avenue, San Francisco, CA 94133
www.citylights.com

PICTURES OF THE GONE WORLD
ANNIVERSARY EDITION

I wrote the twenty-seven poems in this book during a very short period in San Francisco shortly after four years in France on the G.I. Bill.

Poem #1 is the very first poem I wrote in San Francisco, living at 339 Chestnut Street. It is a very North Beach rooftop scene, although it is rife with old-time religious symbolism. During my years in Paris I spent many hours one dark winter with a Jesuit priest who assured me he could make me believe in God without a "leap of faith." (He did not, and I refused to leap.)

Looking back at these poems sixty years later, I see them as written by a new arrival in San Francisco, with a few backward looks to Europe, yet attuned to the unique San Francisco consciousness of the 1950s. And there is a freshness of perception that only young eyes have, in the dandelion bloom of youth.

— LF

Contents

1

Away above a harborful
                              of caulkless houses
among the charley noble chimneypots
                              of a rooftop rigged with clotheslines
          a woman pastes up sails
                              upon the wind
     hanging out her morning sheets
                                   with wooden pins
          O lovely mammal
                              her nearly naked breasts
               throw taut shadows
                              when she stretches up
     to hang at last the last of her
                              so white washed sins
          but it is wetly amorous
                              and winds itself about her
          clinging to her skin
                              So caught with arms upraised
     she tosses back her head
                              in voiceless laughter
     and in choiceless gesture then
                              shakes out gold hair

while in the reachless seascape spaces

          between the blown white shrouds

     stand out the bright steamers

                              to kingdom come

2

Just as I used to say
                    love comes harder to the aged
because they've been running
                    on the same old rails too long
and then when the sly switch comes along
                                they miss the turn
        and burn up the wrong rail while
                        the gay caboose goes flying
        and the steamengine driver don't recognize
                        them new electric horns
and the aged run out on the rusty spur
                            which ends up in
                    the dead grass where
        the rusty tincans and bedsprings and old razor
                    blades and moldy mattresses
                                        lie
        and the rail breaks off dead
                            right there
        though the ties go on awhile
                            and the aged
        say to themselves
                    Well
                    this must be the place
            we were supposed to lie down

And they do

        while the bright saloon careens along away
on a high
    hilltop
        its windows full of bluesky and lovers
  with flowers
          their long hair streaming
            and all of them laughing
     and waving and
         whispering to each other
  and looking out and
          wondering what that graveyard
   where the rails end
        is

In hintertime Praxiteles
               laid about him with a golden maul
striking into stone
             his alabaster ideals
uttering all
        the sculptor's lexicon
                 in visible syllables
   He cast bronze trees
           petrified a chameleon on one
   made stone doves
          fly
           His calipers measured bridges
      and lovers
        and certain other superhumans whom
he caught upon their dusty way
             to death

   They never reached it then

              You still can almost see
      their breath
          Their stone eyes staring
thru three thousand years
         allay our fears of aging

   although Praxiteles himself
         at twenty-eight lay dead

for sculpture isn't for

                young men

as Constantin Brancusi

            at a later hour

      said

4

In Paris in a loud dark winter

       when the sun was something in Provence

when I came upon the poetry

       of René Char

    I saw Vaucluse again

        in a summer of sauterelles

  its fountains full of petals

       and its river thrown down

through all the burnt places

      of that almond world

and the fields full of silence

      though the crickets sang

  with their legs

     And in the poet's plangent dream I saw

no Lorelei upon the Rhone

      nor angels debarked at Marseilles

but couples going nude into the sad water

    in the profound lasciviousness of spring

in an algebra of lyricism

    which I am still deciphering

Not too long

after the beginning of time

upon a nine o'clock

of a not too hot

summer night

standing in the door

of the NEW PISA

under the forgotten

plaster head of DANTE

waiting for a table

and watching

Everything

was a man with a mirror for a head

which didn't look so abnormal at that

except that

real ears stuck out

and he had a sign

which read

A POEM IS A MIRROR WALKING DOWN A STRANGE STREET

but anyway

as I was saying

not too long after the beginning

of time

this man who was all eyes

had no mouth

All he could do was show people

what he meant

And it turned out

he claimed to be

a painter

But anyway

this painter

who couldn't talk or tell anything

about what he

meant

looked like just about the happiest painter

in all the world

standing there

taking it all 'in'

and reflecting

Everything

in his great big

Hungry Eye

but anyway

so it was I saw reflected there

Four walls covered with pictures

of the leaning tower of Pisa

all of them leaning in different directions

Five booths with tables

Fifteen tables without booths

One bar
        with one bartender looking like a
                    baseball champ
          with a lot of naborhood trophies
             hung up behind

Three waitresses of various sizes and faces
          one as big as a little fox terrier
          one as large as a small sperm whale
          one as strange as an angei
       but all three
          with the same eyes
     One kitchendoor with one brother cook
                standing in it
          with the same eyes

               and about
one hundredandsixtythree people all talking and
waving and laughing and eating and drinking and
smiling and frowning and shaking heads and opening
mouths and putting forks and spoons in them and
chewing and swallowing all kinds of produce and
sitting back and relaxing maybe and drinking coffee
and lighting cigarettes and getting up and so on
                and so off

into the night

without ever noticing

the man with the mirrorhead

below the forgotten

plasterhead of DANTE

looking down

at everyone

with the same eyes

as if he were still searching

Everywhere

for his lost Beatrice

but with just a touch

of devilish lipstick

on the very tip

of his nose

And the Arabs asked terrible questions
and the Pope didn't know what to say and the people
ran around in wooden shoes asking which way was the
head of Midas facing and everyone said

No instead of Yes

While still forever in the Luxembourg
gardens in the fountains of the Medici were the
fat red goldfish and the fat white goldfish
and the children running around the pool
pointing and piping
Des poissons rouges!
Des poissons rouges!

but they ran off
and a leaf unhooked itself
and fell upon the pool
and lay like an eye winking
circles

and then the pool was very

                        still
                        and there was a dog
            just standing there
                        at the edge of the pool
                looking down
                        at the tranced fish
        and not barking
                    or waving its funny tail or
                            anything

            so that

                for a moment then

        in the late November dusk

    silence hung like a lost idea
                        and a statue turned

            its head

7

Yes
and we stood about
up in Central Park
dropping coins in the fountains
and a harlequin
came naked among
the nursemaids
and caught them picking their noses
when they should have been

dancing

8

Sarolla's women in their picture hats
stretched upon his canvas beaches
                                    beguiled the Spanish
                        Impressionists

                        And were they fraudulent
                                                pictures
of the world
                the way the light played on them
                                        creating illusions
        of love?

                I cannot help but think
                                    that their 'reality'
was almost as real as
                my memory of today

            when the last sun hung on the hills
            and I heard the day falling
            like the gulls that fell
                        almost to land

        while the last picnickers lay
                        and loved in the blowing yellow broom
resisted and resisting
                    tearing themselves apart
                                        again

                                        again

                    until the last hot hung climax
which could at last no longer be resisted
                                        made them moan

            And night's trees stood up

9

'Truth is not the secret of a few'
                                    yet
you would maybe think so
                    the way some
            librarians
    and cultural ambassadors and
                        especially museum directors
                                                act

    you'd think they had a corner
                            on it
            the way they
                        walk around shaking
    their high heads and
                    looking as if they never
    went to the bath
                room or anything

        But I wouldn't blame them
    if I were you
                They say the Spiritual is best conceived
        in abstract terms
                    and then too
            walking around in museums always makes me
            want to
                    'sit down'
            I always feel so
                            constipated
        in those
                high altitudes

for all I know maybe she was happier
                                        than anyone
that lone crone in the shawl
                        on the orangecrate train
        with the little tame bird
                        in her handkerchief
            crooning
                    to it all the time
                                    mia mascotta

    mia mascotta
                    and none of the sunday excursionists
                        with their bottles and their baskets
                        paying any
                                attention
        and the coach
                    creaking on through cornfields
            so slowly that

                        butterflies

                blew in and out

11

Fortune

           has its cookies to give out

which is a good thing

               since it's been a long time since

         that summer in Brooklyn
      when they closed off the street
           one hot day
            and the

          FIREMEN

                turned on their hoses
and all the kids ran out in it

       in the middle of the street

and there were

           maybe a couple dozen of us

                    out there
with the water squirting up

         to the

            sky

              and all over

                 us

there was maybe only six of us

                      kids altogether

     running around in our

                 barefeet and birthday

   suits

       and I remember Molly but then

the firemen stopped squirting their hoses

      all of a sudden and went

          back in

          their firehouse

           and

      started playing pinochle again

        just as if nothing

         had ever

              happened

while I remember Molly

           looked at me and

  ran in

because I guess really we were the only ones there

And she 'like a young year
>   walking thru the earth'
in the Bois de Boulogne that time
>   or as I remember her
>   stepping out of a bathtub
>   in that gold flat she had
>   corner of
>   *Boulevard des Italiens*

>   Oh they say she tried everything
>   before the end
took up television and crosswords
>   even crocheting
>   and things like that
>   and came to have the air
>   before the end
>   (as her favorite poet described her)
of 'always carrying flowers
>   toward some far
>   abandoned tomb'

which doesn't surprise me now
>   that I come to think of it

>   The struck seed was in her

It was a face which darkness could kill
                                in an instant
    a face as easily hurt
                    by laughter or light

    'We *think* differently at night'
                            she told me once
lying back languidly

                    And she would quote Cocteau

'I feel there is an angel in me' she'd say
                    'whom I am constantly shocking'

    Then she would smile and look away
            light a cigarette for me
                            sigh and rise
and stretch
            her sweet anatomy

                    let fall a stocking

14

So
       he sed
               You think yer pretty snappy
don't you now
               with your sunnyside layer up
           and your bloomin big tits like flowers
           and your way of always looking so inno
                                       cent
           holding a flower between your teeth and
                               laughing with your

       eyes

           Well
               maybe we cud go somewheres
                               (he sed)
       after th'show

funny fantasies are never so real as oldstyle romances
    where the hero has a heroine who has
        long black braids and lets
                    nobody
  kiss her ever
         and everybody's trying all the time to
run away with her
        and the hero is always drawing his
  (sic) sword and
        tilting at ginmills and
                forever telling her he
  loves her and has only honorable intentions and
honorable mentions
         and no one ever beats him at
                    anything
     but then finally one day
        she who has always been so timid
offs with her glove and says
         (though not in so many big words)
    Let's lie down somewheres

             baby

Three maidens went over the land
One carried a piece of bread
                              in the hand
One said
              Let's divide it and cut it

And they strolled thru a red forest
and in the red forest
                        there stood a red church
and in the red church
                        stood a red altar
and upon the red altar
                        lay a red knife
and now we come to the parable
                                They
took the red knife and wounded
                              their bread
and where they cut with the
                        so red knife

                                it was red

Terrible

        a horse at night

    standing hitched alone

             in the still street

      and whinnying

           as if some sad nude astride him

had gripped hot legs on him

          and sung

             a sweet high hungry

      single syllable

18

London

    crossfigured
    creeping with trams

and the artists on sundays
          in the summer
all 'tracking Nature'
       in the suburbs

    It
      could have been anyplace
        but it wasn't
        It was
           London

    and when someone shouted over

that they had got a model

       I ran out across the court

    but then
      when the model started taking off
   her clothes
     there was nothing underneath
        I mean to say
she took off her shoes
       and found no feet
    took off her top
       and found no tit
     under it

and I must say she did look

                              a bit

                                        ASTOUNDED

              just standing there
                    looking down
              at where her legs were

                                        not

But so very carefully then
                              she put her clothes back on
and as soon as she was dressed again

                                        completely

              she was completely

                                        all right

          Do it again! cried someone
                              rushing for his easel

          But she was afraid to

                              and gave up modelling

          and forever after

                    slept in her clothes

with bells for hooves in sounding streets

that terrible horse the unicorn

came on

and cropped a medlar from a tree
                    and where he dropped the seed
sprang up a virgin

                    oh she sprang up upon his back
and rode off tittering to a stair
                    where pieces of string lay scattered
everywhere

          Now when she saw the string so white
so lovely and so beautiful
                    and looking like
                              Innocence itself
she got down and reached for a nice
                              straight piece

          but it had a head
          and it bit
                    her beautiful place

                              So (she said)

this is how it all began

                              Next time I'll know

But it was too late and they buried her

That fellow on the boattrain who insisted
on playing blackjack
had teeth that stuck out
like lighthouses on a rocky coast

but
he had no eyes to see
the dusk flash past

horses in orchards
noiselessly running
bunches of birds
thrown up

and the butterflies of yesterday
that flittered on
my mind

21

Heaven

        was only half as far that night

at the poetry recital

        listening to the burnt phrases

when I heard the poet have

        a rhyming erection

then look away with a

        lost look

'Every animal' be said at last

'After intercourse is sad'

But the back-row lovers

        looked oblivious

and glad

crazy

      to be alive in such a strange

              world

with the band playing schmaltz

            in the classic bandshell

              and the people

   on the benches under the clipped trees

             and girls

  on the grass

        and the breeze blowing and the streamers

streaming

   and a fat man with a graflex

   and a dark woman with a dark dog she called

             Lucia

   and a cat on a leash

   and a pekinese with a blond baby

   and a cuban in a fedora

   and a bunch of boys posing for a group

             picture

and just then

   while the band went right on playing

          schmaltz

a midget ran past shouting and waving his hat

           at someone

   and a young man with a gay campaignbutton

came up and said

      Are you by any chance a registered

        DEMOCRAT?

Dada would have liked a day like this
                         with its various very realistic
              unrealities
                    each about to become
    too real for its locality
                    which is never quite remote enough
       to be Bohemia

Dada would have loved a day like this
                              with its light-bulb sun
         which shines so differently
                         for different people
    but which still shines the same
                              on everyone
                    and on everything
                              such as

       a bird on a bench about to sing

                         a plane in a gilded cloud

a dishpan hand
              waving at a window

                    or a phone about to ring

         or a mouth about to give up
                         smoking

or a new newspaper
               with its new news story
                         of a cancerous dancer

Yes Dada would have died for a day like this
                    with its sweet street carnival
        and its too real funeral
                         just passing thru it
    with its real dead dancer
                    so beautiful and dumb
          in her shroud
                         and her last lover lost
        in the unlonely crowd
                    and its dancer's darling baby
      about to say Dada
                    and its passing priest
        about to pray
                    Dada
                    and offer his so transcendental
          apologies

Yes Dada would have loved a day like this
                         with its not so accidental
          analogies

Picasso's acrobats epitomize the world

and there were eighty churches in Paris

which I

had never entered

and my hotel's door

smiled terribly

and words were trombones

incoherent parrots

chattering idols

but that night I dreamt of Picasso

opening doors and closing exits

opening doors and closing exits in the world

I dreamt

he painted a Picasso

in my room

shouting all the time

Pas symbolique!

C'est pas

symbolique!

The world is a beautiful place
                            to be born into
if you don't mind happiness
                 not always being
                           so very much fun
if you don't mind a touch of hell
                     now and then
just when everything is fine
                       because even in heaven
they don't sing
                 all the time

The world is a beautiful place
                          to be born into
if you don't mind some people dying
                   all the time

or maybe only starving
                     some of the time
which isn't half so bad
               if it isn't you

Oh the world is a beautiful place
                              to be born into
          if you don't much mind
                         a few dead minds
              in the higher places
                         or a bomb or two
              now and then
                         in your upturned faces
     or such other improprieties
                              as our Name Brand society
                    is prey to
                         with its men of distinction
          and its men of extinction
                         and its priests
               and other patrolmen

                              and its various segregations
     and congressional investigations
                              and other constipations
          that our fool flesh
                         is heir to

Yes the world is the best place of all
                           for a lot of such things as
          making the fun scene
                           and making the love scene
and making the sad scene
          and singing low songs and having inspirations
          and walking around
                    looking at everything
                              and smelling flowers
          and goosing statues
                    and even thinking
                              and kissing people and
          making babies and wearing pants
                              and waving hats and
          dancing
                    and going swimming in rivers
               on picnics
                    in the middle of the summer
          and just generally
                    'living it up'

     Yes
          but then right in the middle of it
                              comes the smiling

                    mortician

Reading Yeats I do not think
                    of Ireland
but of midsummer New York
                    and of myself back then
    reading that copy I found
                    on the Thirdavenue El

        the El
                with its flyhung fans
    and its signs reading
                    SPITTING IS FORBIDDEN

        the El
                careening thru its thirdstory world
    with its thirdstory people
                    in their thirdstory doors
    looking as if they had never heard
                            of the ground

        an old dame
                        watering her plant
    or a joker in a straw

                    putting a stickpin in his peppermint tie
and looking just like he had nowhere to go
                                        but coneyisland

              or an undershirted guy
                              rocking in his rocker
watching the El pass by
                as if he expected it to be different
          each time

              Reading Yeats I do not think
                              of Arcady
and of its woods which Yeats thought dead
                                  I think instead
          of all the gone faces
                      getting off at midtown places
      with their hats and their jobs
          and of that lost book I had
                      with its blue cover and its white inside
where a pencilhand had written
                          HORSEMAN, PASS BY!

sweet and various the woodlark

      who sings at the unbought gate

and yet how many

      wild beasts

          how many mad

   in the civil thickets

       Hölderlin

          in his stone tower

or in that kind carpenter's house

       at Tübingen

    or then Rimbaud

       his 'nightmare and logic'

a sophism of madness

But we have our own more recent

       who also fatally assumed

that some direct connection

      does exist between

    language and reality

      word and world

   which is a laugh

      if you ask me

I too have drunk and seen

     the spider